Into I.T.

LEVEL 5

Written by: Laura Miller
Series Editor: Melanie Williams

T0385836

Pearson Education Limited
Edinburgh Gate, Harlow,
Essex CM20 2JE, England
and Associated Companies throughout the world.

ISBN: 978-1-4082-8842-9

This edition first published by Pearson Education Ltd 2014
9 10
Text copyright © Pearson Education Ltd 2014

The moral rights of the author have been asserted
in accordance with the Copyright Designs and Patents Act 1988

Set in 15/19pt OT Fiendstar
Printed in Great Britain by Ashford Colour Press Ltd.
SWTC/02

Acknowledgements
The publisher would like to thank the following for their kind permission to reproduce their photographs:
(Key: b-bottom; c-centre; l-left; r-right; t-top)

Alamy Images: David J. Green - lifestyle themes 13 (2000s), North Wind Picture Archives 13tr,
Pixellover RM 4 13 (2010s), Jochen Tack 6b, travellinglight 11b; **BananaStock:** 25l; **Corbis:** Najlah Feanny 19c,
Robert Galbraith / Reuters 23t, Kim Kulish 22b, Underwood & Underwood 13 (1876); **Fotolia.com:** amor_kar 14tr,
Simone van den Berg 27t, Mariusz Blach 14tl, Vitaliy Bondarchuk 13 (1990s), gradt 14bc, Sergey Ilin 14cr,
Vlad Ivantcov 14br, jamdesign 9t, manaemedia 14tc, Edyta Pawlowska 14cl, Roman Samokhin 14bl; **Getty Images:**
ChinaFotoPress 21t, Phillipe Desmazes / AFP 22t, Neil Farrin 4l, Peter Foley / Bloomberg 23b, John Rowley 8,
Eric Sander 24t, SSPL / Science Museum 18b; **Google and the Google logo are registered trademarks of Google
Inc., used with permission.:** 9c, 9b; **Pearson Education Ltd:** Coleman Yuen 13 (1950s); **PhotoDisc:** Jules Frazier
12c; **Reuters:** Philippe Wojazer 24b; **Rex Features:** Everett Collection 18t, KPA / Zuma 19b, 21b, Nara Archives 29b;
Science Photo Library Ltd: Tim Davies 19t, Patrick Landmann 29t, NASA 15b; **Shutterstock.com:**
Franck Boston 11, Robyn Butler 27, Fotostic 26, Victoria Kisel 1, Milos Luzanin 13 (1980s), Dorottya Mathe 25r,
oleschwander 11c, Rufous 12b, valzan 11tl, ZouZou 4r; **Sozaijiten:** 12t; **SuperStock:** Tetra Images 6t,
Westend61 7; **TopFoto:** 15t, 17, The National Archives / HIP 16b, ullsteinbild 16t
Cover images: *Front:* **SuperStock**: Westend61; *Back:* **Shutterstock.com:** Victoria Kisel

All other images © Pearson Education

Illustrations: Leo Broadley

Published by Pearson Education Ltd

For a complete list of the titles available in the Pearson English Kids Readers series, please go to
www.pearsonenglishkidsreaders.com. Alternatively, write to your local Pearson Education office or to
Pearson English Readers Marketing Department, Pearson Education, Edinburgh Gate, Harlow, Essex CM20 2JE, England.

Contents

Cyberspace!

Some people say, 'Bigger is better.'
What do you say?

In information technology – usually called
I.T. – it is often the opposite. Smaller
things are better because you can carry
them easily. Most people want to have an
I.T. device in their pocket. Why? Because
an I.T. device can take you to cyberspace
– the world of information!

Information technology lets you store
information in cyberspace and helps you
to communicate across cyberspace.

Cyberspace is a virtual world. This means that you cannot touch it or feel it. You can only see it through an I.T. device.

smartphone

Computers and smartphones are I.T. devices, and they take you to cyberspace by going online. To go online, they connect to the Internet. The Internet is a network of millions of computers which can share information. When you connect to the Internet, your life online in cyberspace can begin.

connect

Life Online

Do you spend time online during the week or at the weekend? Maybe your family has a computer at home. Or maybe you use a computer at school. If you go online, what do you do?

Do you send and read emails? Maybe you talk to friends and family in another country. Some people like to watch videos or listen to music online. Other people study or look at photos. There are so many things to do online.

You can find out what the weather is like online without looking outside. You can read the news without buying a newspaper. You can watch a film without going to the cinema, and read a story without opening a book!

To do all these things online, you must visit different websites. Websites are pages of information, and there are millions of websites in cyberspace. All together they are called the World Wide Web (WWW).

The WWW is wonderful for shopping online. You can buy clothes, food, cameras ... just about anything, without leaving home! This is very helpful for people with disabilities who cannot walk or drive easily to the shops.

All online shops are websites, and every website has a web address which starts with 'www'. To go to a website, you go to its web address. We use search engines to find web addresses.

Search engines can help you to find anything on the WWW. For example, students can find out more about their school subjects online. The WWW has an answer for most questions!

Google is a famous search engine. Many people say that they are 'googling' when they are looking for something on the WWW.

Did you 'google' anything today? Think about your life online. What did people do before they had the Internet?

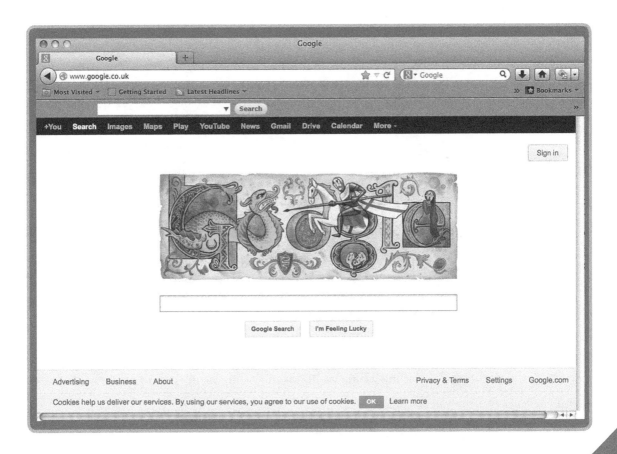

Then and Now

People lived without the Internet for a long time. I.T. is a new science. It is less than 100 years old. The Internet is younger! Most people only started to go online in the 1990s.

But storing and sharing information is nothing new. People started to do it when they started to write – about 5,000 years ago.

Today, we just store and share information in different ways.

In the past, people wrote books by hand. This took a long time! There was usually only one copy of each book, so people looked after books very carefully in a few important libraries.

Later, people printed books, and there were more copies and more libraries. More people learnt to read, and they borrowed books from the libraries. Libraries stored information, so people with questions went to libraries.

Today, people go online. The Internet is now the world's biggest library.

Which is easier – writing or touching something?

In the past, people could only write letters by hand with a pen or pencil on paper. Later, they could use a typewriter. Letters travel in paper envelopes with stamps. They usually take days to arrive.

I.T. changed everything.

Today, you can text on mobile phones, email on computers or text and email from a smartphone. You only have to touch the screen. And your text arrives seconds after you send it.

I.T. also changed how we speak to people.

Alexander Graham Bell invented the telephone in 1876. Before this, you could only talk to a person who was close enough to hear you.

1876

1950s

1980s

1990s

2000s

Early telephones had wires. Most people only started to carry mobile phones in the 1990s. But calling people in other countries was expensive.

Then came Skype. Now we can call for free on the Internet!

2010s

There are many more examples of how I.T. changed our lives. It changed how we work with numbers and how we listen to music. And it changed how we remember what people look like. I.T. is also changing – all the time!

I.T. devices are getting smaller and faster, and they can do more and more. A smartphone today can be a camera, a book and a torch.

And that's just the start! What will it be tomorrow?

The History of I.T.

Before we look at I.T.'s future, let's study its history.

History is full of firsts. In 1964, Jerrie Mock became the first woman to fly round the world. In 1969, Neil Armstrong became the first man on the moon. And I.T. helped them!

Jerrie had a radio to help her to communicate from her plane. Neil used a computer called an AGC.

But what was the first computer? And what did it look like?

In 1941, Konrad Zuse built the Z3 computer in Germany. It helped the Germans to build strong plane wings. In the same year, the ABC computer helped scientists to answer maths problems in the USA.

Konrad Zuse

Colossus

Tommy Flowers built Colossus in 1943. This computer helped the Allies to win the Second World War by reading Germany's secret communications. The name of this computer means 'very, very big'. Was it a good name?

In 1946, John Maunchly and John Eckert built ENIAC. This computer was more like computers today because it could do many different things. But it was still as big as a room!

The Ferranti Mark 1 was much smaller. In 1951, it became the first computer which businesses could buy. It could do many helpful things like answering maths problems. It could also play 'Baa Baa Black Sheep' and easy chess – the first computer game.

Ferranti Mark 1 computer

Through the 1950s and 1960s, computers became smaller and faster. This was thanks to new hardware (computer parts like microchips) and software (programs which tell computers what to do).

In the 1970s, personal computers (PCs) became possible. In 1975, a business called Microsoft started selling computer programs which helped people to use computers more easily. More people started buying PCs.

The next step was a PC which could travel. The first laptop computers came on the market in the early 1980s.

A 1980s laptop

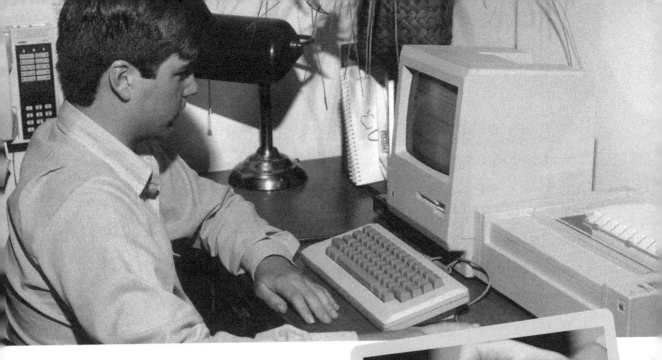

In 1984, a business called Apple sold the first Apple PC. But the Internet was the biggest thing to happen in I.T. in the 1980s.

By connecting computer networks round the world, the Internet made email and the WWW possible. During the 1990s, the number of people using the Internet grew and grew.

Then came the smartphone! The 2002 BlackBerry was the first. Then in 2007, came Apple's iPhone. The iPhone quickly became one of the world's best-selling smartphones.

Who's Who?

How many websites and I.T. businesses do you know?

If you spend time online, you will know a lot!

But do you know the people who started them? Maybe not. In I.T., you spend more time looking at screens than at the faces behind the screens.

Many famous people in I.T. were just students when they started their websites and businesses. Most of them are now very, very rich!

Bill Gates is one of the world's richest people. He started Microsoft, the business which is famous for making Windows software for PCs. Bill learnt about I.T. when his school's Mothers' Club bought an early computer for the students.

Steve Jobs made Apple famous round the world with the iPod, iPhone and iPad. He also started Pixar which made the film 'Toy Story'. Steve liked technology from an early age. His dad taught him how to build radios and TVs.

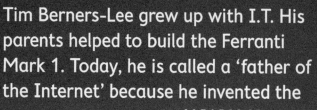

Tim Berners-Lee grew up with I.T. His parents helped to build the Ferranti Mark 1. Today, he is called a 'father of the Internet' because he invented the WWW. He made it free because he wanted all people – rich and poor – to use it.

Larry Page and Sergey Brin helped us to find things on the WWW. In 1998, they started the search engine, Google. The name comes from 'googol', which is the number 10,000,000,000,000,000,000, 000,000,000,000,000,000, 000,000,000,000,000,000, 000,000,000,000,000,000, 000,000,000,000,000,000, 000,000,000!

Larry Page

Sergey Brin

Many websites help us to communicate with friends and have fun. But these websites do not always make money. Mark Zuckerberg started Facebook in 2005, and soon millions of people knew about it.

But it was Sheryl Sandberg who made Facebook a big business.

In 2008, Google and Facebook wanted to hire Sheryl. She chose Facebook. She put clever advertising on the website, and the business started to make money in just two years.

Advertising also helps Yahoo! and YouTube to make money.

David Filo and Jerry Yang started Yahoo! in 1994. They first named their website 'Jerry and David's Guide to the World Wide Web'.

David Filo

Jerry Yang

Steve Chen, Chad Hurley and Jawed Karim started a website for sharing videos in 2005. They called it YouTube. In 2013, people put about 72 hours of video onto YouTube every minute!

The Internet can make people rich and famous. But it can also hurt people.

Chad Hurley

Steve Chen

Danger!

You love being online. But criminals also love being online! How do you know if a person is a criminal online? Do they look like this?

No! People choose how they look on the Internet. A criminal can choose a friendly picture.

Do not believe everything you see on the Internet. Online criminals steal money and identities. And the worst criminals want to hurt children. Always tell your parents if a new online 'friend' wants to meet you.

Cyberspace can be bad in other ways.

Is it a good idea to sit in front of your computer all day? No!

It is important to exercise and spend time outside. More and more children are getting fat because they do not move enough. Playing football is exercise. Playing computer games is not.

It is also important to communicate outside of cyberspace. Talk to your friends. Do not always sit together playing on your phones!

I.T. saves time, but it also wastes time! Many people look at Facebook or YouTube when they have work to do. Always do your work first.

If you have no work to do, then why not read a book, make a cake or throw a ball for your dog?

Remember that 70% of the people in the world today DO NOT have computers or smartphones which can take them to cyberspace. And they still have fun!

The Future

In I.T., the question is always, 'What next?' Computer scientists are working on new hardware and software all the time.

Right now, scientists are trying to make I.T. more like the world outside of cyberspace.

If you look at a photo of a carpet on your computer, can you feel it? No. You can touch the screen, but not the carpet. Scientists are working on screens which will let you feel what you are looking at.

I.T. will become more important in medicine. There are already computers and robots which help with surgery. Maybe a 'RoboDoc' will save your life one day!

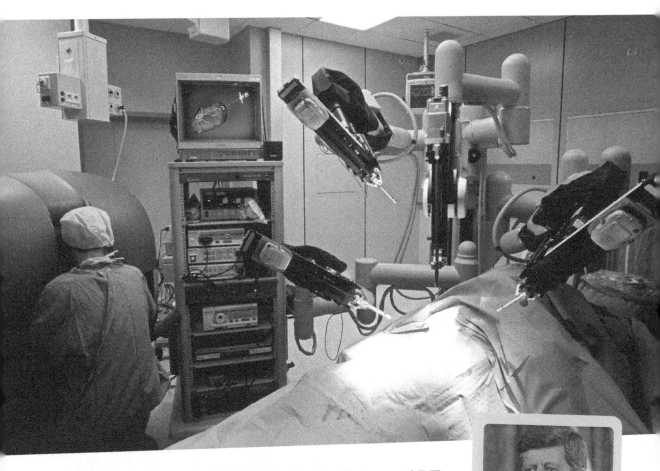

There are wonderful things in the future of I.T. But we must never forget that people are more important than technology.

John F. Kennedy was the President of the USA in the early 1960s when I.T. started to grow. He said something very true, 'Man is still the most extraordinary computer of all.'

Glossary

communicate (v) page 4   to share information by talking, writing, emailing etc.

cyberspace (n) page 4   the world of information online

device (n) page 4   a small thing which does something, e.g. a smartphone

hardware (n) page 18   computer parts that you can see and touch

information (n) page 4   what people know about different subjects

laptop (n) page 18   a small pc which you can carry easily

microchip (n) page 18   a very small electronic part of a computer

network (n) page 5   computers which are connected together to share information

online (adj) page 5   to go online means to connect to the Internet

personal (adj) page 18   for one person to use, e.g. a personal computer

search engine (n) page 8   an Internet program which helps you find information

share (v) page 5   to let other people use or see something which is yours

smartphone (n) page 5   a phone which can go online, take photos, email, etc.

software (n) page 18   computer programs which tell computers what to do

store (v) page 4   to put or keep something somewhere, e.g. books in a library, information on the World Wide Web

technology (n) page 4   a science subject

virtual (adj) page 5   something which you can communicate with but not touch

website (n) page 7   a number of webpages that go together on the World Wide Web

Before You Read

1 **Look at the cover.**
   What is this book about?

   a Flying to another world
   b Computers and information
   c Words and numbers

2 **Complete the sentences with the words**
   below. Use a dictionary to help you.

> information   Internet   email   laptop   communicate   online

   a There is a lot of _____ on I.T. in this book.
   b He is writing an _____ to his friend.
   c I can't go _____ because my computer is not working.
   d You can _____ with your friends by calling them on the phone.
   e If you have a question, you can find the answer on the _____.
   f A _____ is a computer which you can carry around with you.

After You Read

1 Match A to B and then write the complete sentences.

A	B
Sheryl Sandberg	... started Microsoft.
Tim Berners-Lee	... started Apple.
Steve Jobs	... made Facebook a big business.
Bill Gates	... flew around the world.
Alexander Graham Bell	... invented the WWW.
Jerrie Mock	... invented the telephone.

2 Copy and complete the timeline.

a Z3   **b** Blackberry   **c** iPhone   **d** Apple PC

1941 _____ → 1984 _____ → 2002 _____ → 2007 _____

3 Are these sentences true or false? Correct them if they are false.

a You can easily see who is a criminal online.

b Computers, smartphones and tablets are all I.T. devices.

c A smartphone can be a torch, a book and a TV.

d Information technology is 5,000 years old.

e John F. Kennedy said that computers are more important than people.